Francis Frith's
AROUND EASTBOURNE

PHOTOGRAPHIC MEMORIES

Francis Frith's
AROUND EASTBOURNE

◆

Martin Andrew

FRITH
BOOK Co

First published in the United Kingdom in 1999 by
Frith Book Company Ltd

British Library Cataloguing in Publication Data

Around Eastbourne
Martin Andrew
ISBN 1-85937-061-6

Frith Book Company Ltd
Frith's Barn, Teffont,
Salisbury, Wiltshire SP3 5QP
Tel: +44 (0) 1722 716 376
Email: frithbook.co.uk

Printed and bound in Great Britain

CONTENTS

FRANCIS FRITH: *Victorian Pioneer*

FRANCIS FRITH, Victorian founder of the world-famous photographic archive, was a complex and multitudinous man. A devout Quaker and a highly successful Victorian businessman, he was both philosophic by nature and pioneering in outlook.

By 1855 Francis Frith had already established a wholesale grocery business in Liverpool, and sold it for the astonishing sum of £200,000, which is the equivalent today of over £15,000,000. Now a multimillionaire, he was able to indulge his passion for travel. As a child he had pored over travel books written by early explorers, and his fancy and imagination had been stirred by family holidays to the sublime mountain regions of Wales and Scotland. 'What a land of spirit-stirring and enriching scenes and places!' he had written. He was to return to these scenes of grandeur in later years to 'recapture the thousands of vivid and tender memories', but with a different purpose. Now in his thirties, and captivated by the new science of photography, Frith set out on a series of pioneering journeys to the Nile regions that occupied him from 1856 until 1860.

INTRIGUE AND ADVENTURE

He took with him on his travels a specially-designed wicker carriage that acted as both dark-room and sleeping chamber. These far-flung journeys were packed with intrigue and adventure. In his life story, written when he was sixty-three, Frith tells of being held captive by bandits, and of fighting 'an awful midnight battle to the very point of surrender with a deadly pack of hungry, wild dogs'. Sporting flowing Arab costume, Frith arrived at Akaba by camel seventy years before Lawrence, where he encountered 'desert princes and rival sheikhs, blazing with jewel-hilted swords'.

During these extraordinary adventures he was assiduously exploring the desert regions bordering the Nile and patiently recording the antiquities and peoples with his camera. He was the first photographer to venture beyond the sixth cataract. Africa was still the mysterious 'Dark Continent', and Stanley and Livingstone's historic meeting was a decade into the future. The conditions for picture taking confound belief. He laboured for hours in his wicker dark-room in the sweltering heat of the desert, while the volatile chemicals fizzed dangerously in their trays. Often he was forced to work in remote tombs and caves where conditions were cooler. Back in London he exhibited his photographs and was 'rapturously cheered' by members of the Royal Society. His reputation as a photographer was made overnight. An eminent modern historian has likened their impact on the population of the time to that on our own generation of the first photographs taken on the surface of the moon.

VENTURE OF A LIFE-TIME

Characteristically, Frith quickly spotted the opportunity to create a new business as a specialist publisher of photographs. He lived in an era of immense and sometimes violent change. For the poor in the early part of Victoria's reign work was a drudge and the hours long, and people had precious little free time to enjoy themselves.

Most had no transport other than a cart or gig at their disposal, and had not travelled far beyond the boundaries of their own town or village. However, by the 1870s, the railways had threaded their way across the country, and Bank Holidays and half-day Saturdays had been made obligatory by Act of Parliament. All of a sudden the ordinary working man and his family were able to enjoy days out and see a little more of the world.

With characteristic business acumen, Francis Frith foresaw that these new tourists would enjoy having souvenirs to commemorate their days out. In 1860 he married Mary Ann Rosling and set out with the intention of photographing every city, town and village in Britain. For the next thirty years he travelled the country by train and by pony and trap, producing fine photographs of seaside resorts and beauty spots that were keenly bought by millions of Victorians. These prints were painstakingly pasted into family albums and pored over during the dark nights of winter, rekindling precious memories of summer excursions.

THE RISE OF FRITH & CO

Frith's studio was soon supplying retail shops all over the country. To meet the demand he gathered about him a small team of photographers, and published the work of independent artist-photographers of the calibre of Roger Fenton and Francis Bedford. In order to gain some understanding of the scale of Frith's business one only has to look at the catalogue issued by Frith & Co in 1886: it runs to some 670

pages, listing not only many thousands of views of the British Isles but also many photographs of most European countries, and China, Japan, the USA and Canada – note the sample page shown above from the hand-written *Frith & Co* ledgers detailing pictures taken. By 1890 Frith had created the greatest specialist photographic publishing company in the world, with over 2,000 outlets – more than the combined number that Boots and WH Smith have today! The picture on the right shows the *Frith & Co* display board at Ingleton in the Yorkshire Dales. Beautifully constructed with mahogany frame and gilt inserts, it could display up to a dozen local scenes.

POSTCARD BONANZA

◆◆

The ever-popular holiday postcard we know today took many years to develop. In 1870 the Post Office issued the first plain cards, with a pre-printed stamp on one face. In 1894 they allowed other publishers' cards to be sent through the mail with an attached adhesive halfpenny stamp. Demand grew rapidly, and in 1895 a new size of postcard was permitted called the

court card, but there was little room for illustration. In 1899, a year after Frith's death, a new card measuring 5.5 x 3.5 inches became the standard format, but it was not until 1902 that the divided back came into being, with address and message on one face and a full-size illustration on the other. *Frith & Co* were in the vanguard of postcard development, and Frith's sons Eustace and Cyril continued their father's monumental task, expanding the number of views offered to the public and recording more and more places in Britain, as the coasts and countryside were opened up to mass travel.

Francis Frith died in 1898 at his villa in Cannes, his great project still growing. The archive he created continued in business for another seventy years. By 1970 it contained over a third of a million pictures of 7,000 cities, towns and villages. The massive photographic record Frith has left to us stands as a living monument to a special and very remarkable man.

Frith's Archive: *A Unique Legacy*

FRANCIS FRITH'S legacy to us today is of immense significance and value, for the magnificent archive of evocative photographs he created provides a unique record of change in 7,000 cities, towns and villages throughout Britain over a century and more. Frith and his fellow studio photographers revisited locations many times down the years to update their views, compiling for us an enthralling and colourful pageant of British life and character.

We tend to think of Frith's sepia views of Britain as nostalgic, for most of us use them to conjure up memories of places in our own lives with which we have family associations. It often makes us forget that to Francis Frith they were records of daily life as it was actually being lived in the cities, towns and villages of his day. The Victorian age was one of great and often bewildering change for ordinary people, and though the pictures evoke an impression of slower times, life was as busy and hectic as it is today.

We are fortunate that Frith was a photographer of the people, dedicated to recording the minutiae of everyday life. For it is this sheer wealth of visual data, the painstaking chronicle of changes in dress, transport, street layouts, buildings, housing, engineering and landscape that captivates us so much today. His remarkable images offer us a powerful link with the past and with the lives of our ancestors.

TODAY'S TECHNOLOGY

Computers have now made it possible for Frith's many thousands of images to be accessed almost instantly. In the Frith archive today, each photograph is carefully 'digitised' then stored on a CD Rom. Frith archivists can locate a single photograph amongst thousands within seconds. Views can be catalogued and sorted under a variety of categories of place and content to the immediate benefit of researchers. Inexpensive reference prints can be created for them at the touch of a mouse button, and a wide range of books and other printed materials assembled and published for a wider, more general readership - in the next twelve months over a hundred Frith local history titles will be published! The

day-to-day workings of the archive are very different from how they were in Francis Frith's time: imagine the herculean task of sorting through eleven tons of glass negatives as Frith had to do to locate a particular sequence of pictures! Yet the archive still prides itself on maintaining the same high standards of excellence laid down by Francis Frith, including the painstaking cataloguing and indexing of every view.

It is curious to reflect on how the internet now allows researchers in America and elsewhere greater instant access to the archive than Frith himself ever enjoyed. Many thousands of individual views can be called up on screen within seconds on one of the Frith internet sites, enabling people living continents away to revisit the streets of their ancestral home town, or view places in Britain where they have enjoyed holidays. Many overseas researchers welcome the chance to view special theme selections, such as transport, sports, costume and ancient monuments.

We are certain that Francis Frith would have heartily approved of these modern developments, for he himself was always working at the very limits of Victorian photographic technology.

THE VALUE OF THE ARCHIVE TODAY

Because of the benefits brought by the computer, Frith's images are increasingly studied by social historians, by researchers into genealogy and ancestory, by architects, town planners, and by teachers and schoolchildren involved in local history projects. In addition, the archive offers every one of us a unique opportunity to examine the places where we and our families have lived and worked down the years. Immensely successful in Frith's own era, the archive is now, a century and more on, entering a new phase of popularity.

THE PAST IN TUNE WITH THE FUTURE

Historians consider the Francis Frith Collection to be of prime national importance. It is the only archive of its kind remaining in private ownership and has been valued at a million pounds. However, this figure is now rapidly increasing as digital technology enables more and more people around the world to enjoy its benefits.

Francis Frith's archive is now housed in an historic timber barn in the beautiful village of Teffont in Wiltshire. Its founder would not recognize the archive office as it is today. In place of the many thousands of dusty boxes containing glass plate negatives and an all-pervading odour of photographic chemicals, there are now ranks of computer screens. He would be amazed to watch his images travelling round the world at unimaginable speeds through network and internet lines.

The archive's future is both bright and exciting. Francis Frith, with his unshakeable belief in making photographs available to the greatest number of people, would undoubtedly approve of what is being done today with his lifetime's work. His photographs, depicting our shared past, are now bringing pleasure and enlightenment to millions around the world a century and more after his death.

EASTBOURNE – *An Introduction*

'THE EMPRESS OF WATERING PLACES'

Eastbourne as we see it now seems always to have been there, but it is a great surprise to find that before about 1850 it barely existed. Unlike most of the other south coast resorts, the 'Empress of Watering Places' developed late. This may seem odd, given its enormous physical advantages, but it comes down to land ownership. Nowadays the bustling town, often awash with French schoolchildren in the summer months as well as other visitors, has a population of over 80,000 and has long swamped the four settlements from which it grew: three, East Bourne, South Bourne and Sea Houses, along the Bourne stream, now largely underground, and one, Meads, to the west.

The two land-owning families hereabouts were the Cavendishes, the family of the Dukes of Devonshire whose principal seat is Chatsworth in Derbyshire, and the Gilberts. The Cavendishes acquired Compton Place and its park, along with large acreages around it, and more importantly much of the coastline. They kept Compton Place as a rural retreat where the stimulating air and sea

bathing was of benefit. It is said that this desire for privacy held back the development of Eastbourne. There is a story that Decimus Burton, the great early 19th-century architect, arrived in 1833 at Compton Place to show the then Cavendish in residence, Lord Burlington, plans for a resort to be called 'Burlington'. He was sent packing, and instead developed St.Leonards, further along the coast near Hastings.

It was not until this Lord Burlington's grandson, William, inherited the title of Duke of Devonshire in 1858 that Eastbourne really got going. It had started before that to some extent, and William had successfully lobbied for a railway line into Eastbourne, the first station opening in 1849. He had Terminus Road laid out, and in 1851 began the Burlington Hotel, Cavendish Place and Victoria Place. After 1858 things moved faster, working to a master plan drawn up by Henry Currey, the Duke's new surveyor. A grand town layout was designed, with great terraces and sea-front ranges. Currey had worked with Decimus Burton and was an inspired choice, as well as being a kinsman of the 'Duke's solicitor. His terraces shaded into elegant gabled villas on land to the north and west between Compton Place, the sea and Beachy Head, absorbing the hamlet of Meads on the way. The Gilberts developed to the east of the Cavendish lands, and this stately, elegant and refined watering place emerged.

Its character is very much later Victorian, for the earliest terraces, such as Cornfield Terrace, the Belle Vue Hotel or the refined Burlington Terrace, owed much to the late Regency flavour of other seaside resorts such as Brighton and Hove. Eastbourne developed a more exuberant range of architecture, rang-

adversely changed this. It is a splendid town, with a great variety of architectural types from 1850 onwards. It has a bustling commercial centre, with Terminus road largely pedestrianised, and many historians consider its skilled layout an exemplar only matched by Bournemouth in seaside resort planning.

And yet it all started out rather curiously. By the end of the 18th century the fashion for seabathing had led to the small fishing hamlet of Sea Houses evolving as a watering place resort. Several houses were built here and one, The Round House, was converted from a

ing from the French Empire-influenced Cavendish, Grand and Queen's Hotels, the Italianate of Lansdowne Terrace to the Jacobethan of the Albion Hotel. The town plan, though, remains a fine one, with terraces, squares and elegantly curved roads. The grid is full of incident and variety, and without much of the obvious regimentation of streets at right angles to each other. The town planning was masterly, and extensive rebuilding, much of it a consequence of bombing in World War II or misplaced ambition of the post-war city fathers, has not

windmill into a house. A royal seal of approval, so important to the development of the south coast watering places, was achieved as early as 1780 when Prince Edward, King George III's son, stayed there. However, little else happened; although Sea Houses acquired a library and a bathhouse in the early 19th century, again essential requisites for a Georgian resort, it remained a small scale resort where sea bathers jostled with the fishermen drying their nets and gutting their catches.

Several of the original Georgian buildings

of Sea Houses remain to the west of the Albion Hotel, while the old village of East Bourne is still recognisable in parts. A disastrously ill-judged road widening took out the south side of the High Street and Church Street, and the demolition of the old Star Brewery in 1973 definitively changed the old town's character. The brewery site is now occupied by a supermarket. However around the church, itself a good medieval one, are a group of outstanding buildings which make the walk uphill from the sea front well worth the effort. Here you can take refreshment at The Lamb Inn, an excellent timber-framed building with a 14th century stone vaulted undercroft. Then move on to look at the Old Parsonage, 16th century with massive chimney stacks, and its barn, dignified by a close-studded upper storey. The Manor House survives as the Towner Art Gallery, and there are other good buildings to counteract the harm done by road widening. In the earlier days of the resort, the old town was an important element in its life. The Lamb Inn, for example, provided assembly rooms for gatherings and balls, and the church was also in the old town. The hamlet of South Bourne provided the theatre: not quite Bath or Brighton.

Returning to the sea-side story, the promenades had been started in the 1840s, as Burlington was concerned at the rapid erosion by the sea. They continued on a much grander scale, as befitted the evolving resort. Indeed, Empress of Watering Places is an excellent nick-name, for it captures exactly the slightly grand, sedate, select and stately, almost matronly, nature of the late Victorian town. Deliberate efforts were made to keep the clientele select and to discourage 'the day tripper or excursionist'.

The necessary facilities for a seaside resort arrived at the same time, the most important being the pier. Designed by Eugenius Birch, it opened in 1870, although started in 1866 and not finished until 1872. Disastrous storms in 1877 led to the landward end having to be rebuilt; subsequently the pier acquired buildings at various times, including a 'Kursaal' at the seaward end, an elaborate fairy-tale palace built around 1900 to replace an earlier simpler one. The name 'kursaal' was adopted from the 'cure hall' of German spa towns, and was intended to exude good health. In 1924 the landward end acquired a large, bulbous-roofed Music Pavilion. The pier remains much as it did in the 1920s; further along the promenade the obligatory bandstand was erected, the well-known 'bird cage'. This was relocated east to the Redoubt Gardens in the 1920s, and a most exotic structure with a bright turquoise dome and faience colonnades replaced the promenade bandstand in 1934. Again, this survives.

Just inland, Devonshire Park began to acquire entertainment buildings, including a theatre in 1884, and a floral hall and winter gardens in the 1870s; the latter is now replaced by the 1950s Congress Theatre. Further west, Henry Currey drew up his second master plan for the areas around Meads. This time, in the 1870s, he moved away from terraces to villas in grounds, a refined development that used the contours well and earned the area the nickname of 'The Belgravia of Eastbourne'.

All this expansion led the Duke, his advisors and the townspeople to lobby for Eastbourne to become a town, rather than a parish. This was eventually successful and a royal charter was granted in 1883. The

Borough of Eastbourne was born, and George Wallis, the Duke's agent, became its first mayor. As befitted its new status a grand Town Hall, designed by a Birmingham architect, opened in 1886 and the town prospered mightily. However, in 1891, the Duke died, and in 1895 Wallis died. The eighth Duke of Devonshire did much for the town, and even became mayor in 1897, but this was in the way of consolidation and completion of earlier schemes. The seventh Duke's era from the 1850s was the key one, and the town's population rose from under six thousand in 1861 to over twenty thousand by 1881 and forty thousand in 1901. In 1911 the town achieved County Borough status, and in 1929 the corporation bought four thousand acres of downland around Beachy Head and up to Polegate - a philanthropic gesture of immense importance to the future of the town and its setting.

The town prospered as a select resort until the Second World War, when it was subject to numerous bombing raids. It has been calculated that 1475 buildings were destroyed or badly damaged, including the Cavendish Hotel and Barclays Bank of 1895 on Terminus Road, while the human toll was equally heavy with about two hundred killed and thirteen hundred injured. After the War there was reconstruction of bomb-damaged buildings, and rapid expansion of the suburbs at Hampden park or Langney brought the town to its present size.

There have been only a few really unfortunate new buildings on the sea-front emerging from the vigour of regeneration. Fortunately, most of the replacement buildings have been no higher than their Victorian predecessors, whatever the bland quality of the many recent blocks of flats. The intrusions are the quite extraordinarily inappropriate Transport and General Workers Union Conference and Holiday Centre - gloomy, out-of-scale, aggressive, wrong-headed and an insult, built in 1975 - and the equally crass eighteen-storey South Cliff Tower block of flats further west and on higher ground. Much of Terminus Road has been reconstructed, partly as a consequence of bombing.

This includes the 1895 Barclays Bank, a fine classical building, and the shops to its west, now under the 1981 Arndale shopping centre.

Following a decline in the holiday trade in the face of package tour competition in the 1960s and 1970s, the town has, as the jargon would put it, 're-focussed', building up a very large conference trade and now catering for the dreaded day-tripper avoided in former years. It has museums and attractions such as The Redoubt, the Napoleonic period fort which houses a military collection, the 'How We Lived Then' museum of Victorian life in Cornfield Terrace, the Butterfly Centre on Royal Parade, the Towner Gallery of course, and the swimming pools and flumes of the Sovereign Centre, while out of town is the Beachy Head Countryside Centre. But despite all the changes that have taken place since the Eighth Duke died in 1908, he would recognise his 'company' town and not be dismayed by what he saw.

The transformation of a fishing village into the bustling architecturally coherent and high-quality town of today is a fascinating story; it took place fundamentally over about half a century, from about 1849 when the railway was persuaded to head for Eastbourne until the early 1900s. Mind you, since the war, and with increasing pace, the town is expanding; recent developments have taken it eastwards towards The Crumbles, where the new Sovereign Harbour and marina gives the town high hopes for the future, whatever might be said about the destruction of the Langney Levels.

When you have tired of the town Chapter 4 takes you up to Beachy Head and its downland and sheer cliffs. The last chapter provides an illustrated itinerary that takes in many of the more interesting features, towns and villages in an arc west, north and east of the town, as far west as the ancient port of Seaford, north to Hailsham, the 'String Town', and east to Pevensey with its remarkably intact 4th century Roman fortress. I hope you enjoy all the chapters, with their view of Eastbourne and its environs spanning the period from the 1890s to the 1960s; they will give a background and interest for your many, I hope, visits to this elegant town.

ON THE SANDS 1910 62959
Obviously, photographing children playing on the beach was a popular theme for postcard makers. On the pier beyond can be seen the cast-iron wind breaks added in 1903 and the Kursaal at the end.

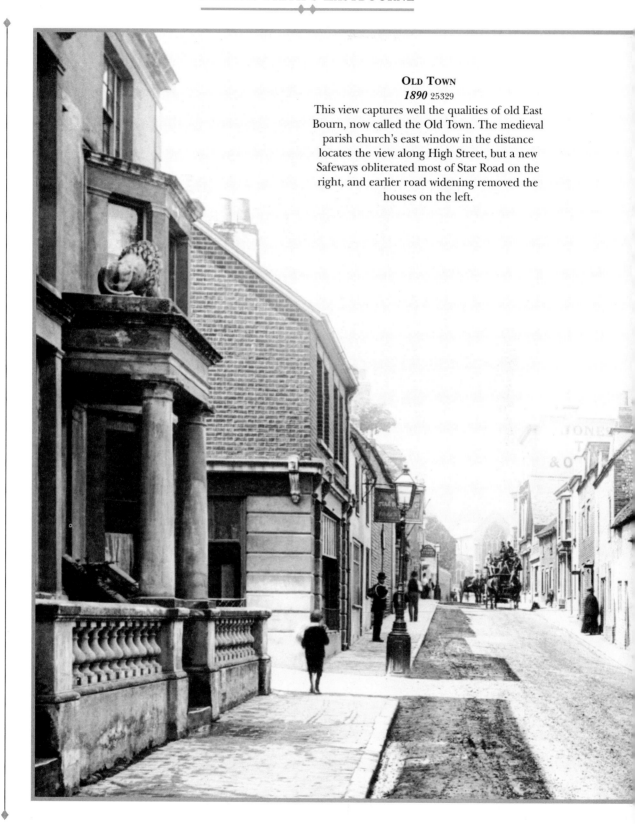

OLD TOWN
1890 25329
This view captures well the qualities of old East Bourn, now called the Old Town. The medieval parish church's east window in the distance locates the view along High Street, but a new Safeways obliterated most of Star Road on the right, and earlier road widening removed the houses on the left.

MEADS ROAD 1890 25313

It is regrettable that all the trees have now gone in this view looking towards the Town Hall, but the flint walls and the house on the right survive. The wall on the left fronts Saffrons Park, now a sports club, with its entrance gates dated 1914. Note the characteristic brick pavements of the fashionable 'Belgravia of Eastbourne'.

MEADS ROAD 1894 34473

Again, the flint walls remain, and the brick pavings on the right survive, but the pillar box on the corner of Blackwater Road has been replaced by a modern one. Some of the trees remain, while there is new housing, Saffrons Park and Court, behind the left hand flint walls, which also survive.

TOWN HALL 1890 25310
Booming expansion led the Duke of Devonshire and the townspeople to lobby for borough status, finally granted by royal charter in June 1883. A design competition for a suitably grand town hall was won by W Tadman Foulkes, a Birmingham architect, and the foundation stone was laid in 1884 by Lord Edward Cavendish, the Duke's son.

TERMINUS ROAD 1925 77962
When the railway arrived in 1849 George Cavendish, Earl of Burlington, laid out Terminus Road to link the station to the sea front, and it rapidly became Eastbourne's main commercial street. In this view from the Gildredge Road junction, looking away from the station, all on the left has since been rebuilt.

TERMINUS ROAD
1925 77963

The road is now pedestrianised and much has been lost in this view. The grand classical building on the left, built in 1895 for the Lewes Old Bank, was bombed in 1943: it is now Barclays Bank. The stucco Royal Hotel at the right, on Cornfield Road corner, was replaced by the present NatWest bank in about 1930.

EASTBOURNE, TERMINUS ROAD 1925 77961
Just past the Midland Bank, looking north west, the elegant late Victorian shops on the left survive, although W H Smith has now moved on. The right-hand terraces with their shop blinds were bombed in 1943, and were replaced by the less interesting Arndale Shopping Centre of 1981.

ALL SOULS CHURCH 1890 25319
Apparently transplanted from Romanesque Italy, this remarkable church in yellow and red brick was funded by the great-niece of the Duke of Wellington, Lady Victoria Wellesley. This view from Tideswell Road shows the 83 feet high 'campanile' or detached bell tower and the semi-circular apse of this 'basilica' church. It remains virtually unaltered.

ALL SOULS CHURCH 1890 25320
This church was one of a number of parish churches built to cater for the expanding town. Designed by Alfred Strong, a London architect, it was built in 1882. The builder was James Peerless, who was also the contractor for the Town Hall.

THE PIER
1901 48065
In the early 1860s the Pier Company was formed, but
infighting slowed the work; Eugenius Birch's pier, started
in 1866 and part-opened in 1870 by Lord Edward
Cavendish, was not completed until 1872. Here, the
earliest entrance kiosk is flanked by later domed ones.

THE PIER 1906 56687

THE PIER 1906
As we look past the children paddling, the seaward end of the pier is terminated by the Kursaal of 1899, replacing a smaller 1888 one that had cost a mere £250. Containing a theatre, bars, offices and tea-rooms, the Kursaal took its name from the fashionable German spa town 'curehalls'.

◆

THE PIER 1912
Taken from the Grand Parade, this view shows well the much-needed 1903 windbreak screen and the higher deck level of the post-1877 rebuilt landward section of the pier, which had been washed away in storms. Arriving at the pier is a full charabanc drawn by three horses.

THE PIER 1912 64968

THE PIER 1925 77946

In 1912 the entrance kiosks were rebuilt with more exotic roofs; beyond is the then new bulbous-roofed Music Pavilion, erected in 1924 at a cost of £15,000. Two smart white-liveried motor charabancs are collecting holiday makers from the pier, possibly for the advertised excursion over the South Downs.

THE PIER c1955 E5129

The Victorian domed kiosk between the mid-saloons and the Kursaal had been removed by the time this view was taken, and the Kursaal itself has since had the left-hand end simplified and the turrets removed.

ROYAL PARADE
1901 48063
Past the Georgian remains of Sea Houses, at
the junction of Royal Parade with Seaside, is
the flamboyant Albion Hotel, now renamed
the Carlton Hotel, its red brick all colour-
washed. It was built in 1887 in a sort of
Dutch/Flemish Renaissance style with ornate
dormers and domed turrets.

THE PROMENADE GARDENS 1912 64974
The famous Carpet Gardens on Grand Parade were laid out between the pier and the bandstand with intricate patterns picked out in bedding plants and taller plants along the outer beds. On the left is one of the finest stucco terraces in Eastbourne, the Burlington and Claremont Hotels of 1851: worthy of Brighton.

GRAND PARADE 1910 62952
Pre-World War I ladies in their elegant dresses parade along the promenade with some protecting themselves from the sun beneath umbrellas. The old bandstand, known locally as the 'bird cage', cost the large sum of £3,000 when it was built in the early 1890s.

GRAND PARADE 1910 62949
More pre-World War I bustle, with the pier in the background looking delicate and graceful without the rather bulbous 1924 music pavilion. On the left is the Chatsworth Hotel of the 1870s, yet another Eastbourne one named after something to do with the Dukes of Devonshire.

GRAND PARADE
1910 62953
The festoons of electric light bulbs were a noted attraction for visitors strolling the promenade in the evenings and for the evening concerts given at the octagonal bandstand, beyond the Cigar Kiosk sign. Not quite the equal of the Blackpool Illuminations, though.

THE PARADE AND BANDSTAND 1899 43942

Seen from Grand Parade, across the lower parade, the old bandstand has its awnings extended to protect the musicians from the sun. The photograph is also interesting as it shows the earlier pier mid-buildings before their reconstruction in 1901, two years after the date of this view.

THE BEACH 1921 71411

Looking at the bandstand from the beach, the reason for its popular name of 'the bird cage' is obvious. It was carried on iron columns which raised it above the promenade, where chairs and an arcaded 'grandstand' catered for the audience.

THE PARADE 1921 77941

By 1925, the music pavilion had been added to the landward end of the pier; while strolling along the promenade remains immensely popular, the folding deck chair has now arrived in large numbers. Some people can be seen using their umbrellas to protect themselves from the sun.

THE PARADE 1925 77940

With fewer people about on a less sunny day, the three tiers of the sea front are clearer to see, with the road and pavement to the left separated from the wide Promenade below by trim hedges. To the right the Lower Promenade, closer to beach level, is separated by a sloping bank of more informal shrubs.

THE BANDSTAND AT THE REDOUBT
1925 77949
After the 'bird cage' bandstand was taken down in about 1934 from its location on Grand Parade, it was moved east to the Redoubt Gardens; it is pictured here with a band in full swing. It has since been demolished, while the Redoubt, a Napoleonic defence fort, is now a military museum.

THE BANDSTAND c1955 E5153

The old 'birdcage' bandstand was replaced in 1934-35 by an altogether grander affair with a seating capacity of three thousand people. This more distant view also shows the columned enclosure that surrounded the 'squashed onion' domed central bandstand which provided an upper gallery of seating, all set on a projection onto the beach.

THE BANDSTAND c1955 E5105

The columned structure of the enclosure and the bandstand itself are faced in buff faience, while the flattened dome over the bandstand is in a startling turquoise blue surmounted by a golden spike. There is much ornamentation, and although the elaborate lamps have now gone, it is still an exotic and striking building.

THE PIER ENTRANCE 1912 64973
The domes of the newly rebuilt pavilions are seen here gleaming in the sunshine. On the far left a statue of a Royal Sussex Regiment soldier looks towards the pier. Sculpted in bronze and erected as a memorial to the regiment, it was unveiled amid great pomp in 1904.

THE PROMENADE c1955 E5184
Eastbourne was still immensely popular in the 1950s before the foreign package holiday boom arrived to threaten its pre-eminence. If we compare this view with the 1920s ones, the clothes still seem remarkably formal, but modern casualness is beginning to arrive with open-neck shirts and even chaps in shirtsleeves.

THE PROMENADE c1965 E5205

The present entrance kiosk building replaced the 1940s one seen in this view with a much more exotic Turkish pavilion, enlarged in 1991. The bright sunlight glares off the stucco of the Belle Vue hotel and the Queen's Hotel beyond.

THE BELLE VUE HOTEL c1965 E5216

All the buildings in this view survive, including the smaller houses in Elms Avenue and the rather good 1850s stucco of the Belle Vue Hotel, with its arched ground floor windows and heavy moulded cornice below the top storey windows.

FROM THE PIER 1906 56684

Behind the crammed Edwardian beach, with boats launched into the millpond of a sea, most of the buildings of Grand Parade survive today, the notable exception being the small gabled house, now replaced. The Cavendish Hotel is the taller building at the left, now dwarfed by the remarkably ill-judged grey mass of the Transport and General Workers Union Holiday and Conference Centre opened in 1976. It replaced the Sea View Hotel, and cost £3 million to build.

THE PARADE
1899 43938
This view shows well the more varied architectural styles after the 1850s compared with the stucco elegance of the Burlington on the right. To the left, beyond the old bandstand, is a good view of the Wish Tower, the Napoleonic period martello tower.

THE BEACH AND PARADE 1925 77939
The central bays of the promenade building survive, but the arched bays on each side were rebuilt in the 1950s.
Kiosks line the promenade selling drinks, snacks, candy floss and all the things necessary for the perfect seaside
holiday.

EASTBOURNE BEACH 1894 34459

The edge of the beach is lined with bathing machines in this view. The Cavendish Hotel, the tall building of 1873 to 1882 with steep French pavilion roofs and a higher central tower, lost its right-hand half to World War II bombs and was rebuilt in insensitive modern slab style.

THE PROMENADE 1912 64976

The Wish Tower, in the distance on the left, was built as a Martello Tower, one of over one hundred round-towered fortlets built along the south coast during the Napoleonic Wars. Named after an admired fortlet in Corsica at Mortella, this one, Number 73, is one of eleven surviving in Sussex.

THE LAWNS 1910 62955

The town climbs increasingly steeply away from the sea to the west of the Wish Tower, with an expansive greensward, known as the Western Lawns, between the muc' lower promenade and the buildings fronting King Edwards Parade. Beyond it lies the wonderful climax of the Downs and Beachy Head.

KING EDWARDS PARADE c1965 E5219

Lansdowne Terrace, now the Lansdowne Hotel, and, at the right, the Wish Tower Hotel, was the first major development west of the Wish Tower; it is in the style of the earlier stucco terraces, with its central pediment and 'palace front' composition. Only the bay windows give away its 1860s date.

THE WESTERN LAWNS 1912 64966
The view looking beyond the Lansdowne Hotel and the Grand Hotel is now dominated by South Cliff Tower, an eighteen-storey block of flats about which the words 'sore thumb' come unbidden to mind: an example of the sort of tower block that all south coast resorts seemed to need.

THE GARDENS AND THE WISH TOWER, 1925 77953

Closer to the sea, the upper promenade climbs east to pass the Wish Tower with the sea now some way below. In front of the Tower, now housing the Coastal Defence Museum, the colonnaded building has been replaced by the present 1960s-style Restaurant and Sun Lounge.

THE WESTERN LAWNS 1925 77951

The statue by Drury that now adorns the Western Lawns was erected by the townsfolk in 1910. It is of Spencer Compton, 8th Duke of Devonshire, who was Mayor of Eastbourne in 1897-98, in effect leader of his own 'company town'. He died in 1908.

THE LANSDOWNE PRIVATE HOTEL c1955 E5155

Lansdowne Terrace, a long Italianate terrace facing the Wish Tower, was built in the 1860s with its centre spanned by a wide triangular pediment; it was soon mostly colonised by the Lansdowne Private Hotel. The rendered range with its straight parapet is in marked contrast to the much more ornate Grand Hotel to its left.

THE BEACH
1901 48061

The tide is in, and the sea is a millpond fringed by
bathing machines in this view looking from the
lawns east of the Wish Tower. On the left is the old
Sea View Hotel, which was replaced in the 1970s by
the dismal tower of the Transport and General
Workers Union Holiday and Conference Centre.

FROM THE WISH TOWER
1899 43935
The coastline bulging out around the Wish Tower
affords a vantage point for views north-east along
the beach; this view shows the horse-drawn bathing
machines on their large wheels plying their trade.
Note the bathing machine horses stand drowsing in
the warm summer sunshine.

GRAND HOTEL 1901 48064

Altogether a grander affair, the hotel opened in the 1870s; it adopted a fashionable French architectural style, marked by a complex roof line with ornate dormer windows in a steep mansarded roof, and pavilion-roofed towers crested with miniature railings: a style suited to the more grandiose tastes of the later Victorian age.

GRAND PARADE 1912 64969

The elegance of this 1860s stucco terrace with three-storey bay windows to each house and the long straight parapet is now replaced by Grand Court, a higher block of 1960s flats: typical sea-front flats that can be found in every seaside resort, and distinctly not enhancing the elegant Victorian character of Eastbourne.

THE BEACH 1925 77936

When we contrast this view with the one taken in 1901, the bathing machines have gone, to be replaced by changing tents and the long lines of beach huts. The pier has acquired the Music Pavilion at the landward end, and the domed bandstand between the Games Saloon and the Kursaal at the seaward end.

FROM THE WISH TOWER 1925 77935

At the far left, the single-storey building is the old lifeboat station of 1898, which in 1937 became the world's first lifeboat museum. It had been built as a memorial to William Terris, a well-known actor murdered at the stage door of London's Adelphi theatre in 1897.

BEACHY HEAD 1910 62961

Beachy Head is where the chalk range of the South Downs reaches the sea in magnificent chalk cliffs rearing almost vertically five hundred feet out of the sea. This view from the clifftop looks down on the lighthouse, itself 153 feet high and reduced to the scale of a toy.

BEACHY HEAD COAST 1910 62962

The rugged nature and scale of the cliffs at Beachy Head, seen here to the east of the lighthouse, is clearly shown in this view. It is amazing that this headland, notoriously dangerous and strewn with shipwrecks down the centuries, did not have any permanent lighthouse until the Belle Tout was erected in 1832.

BEACHY HEAD FROM THE SANDS 1903
This tranquil view from the sands, taken a year after the lighthouse was completed, shows the rock-strewn shelf along the foot of the soaring cliffs. These cliffs, though, are dangerous: early in 1999 five thousand tons of chalk fell, temporarily linking the lighthouse to the land, until washed away by the surging tides and currents.

◆

BEACHY HEAD 1912 64982
The lighthouse, started in 1899, replaced the Belle Tout on the cliff top further west. A remarkable operation, it was built on massive foundations using Cornish granite. Opened in 1902 with its striking red and white painted bands, it was constantly manned until automated in 1983.

BEACHY HEAD FROM THE SANDS 1903 50417

BEACHY HEAD 1912 64982

FROM BEACHY HEAD 1910 62942
This view, now on the South Downs Way long distance footpath, looks down towards Eastbourne past Meads. In the foreground are the buildings of St Bede's School, while to the left the long building is All Saints Hospital, founded in 1867 by an Anglican nun, and built in Victorian Gothic style.

THE CONVALESCENT HOME 1891 29692
Immediately south of her All Saints Hospital, the Reverend Mother Harriet built this imposing convalescent home, also in the Victorian Gothic style. Meads and the slopes leading up to the Downs and Beachy Head were considered ideally healthy, and convalescent homes and large villas proliferated: it used to be known as Eastbourne's Belgravia.

HOLY WELL FROM ABOVE 1894 34475
By 1894 the Meads area is filling up with villas. The grassy sward in the foreground is now the Helen Garden, and the middle distance is dominated by South Cliff Tower, an unfortunate eighteen-storey block of flats built in 1966 that sits ill amid the villas, which are now themselves being replaced by lower blocks of flats.

THE HELEN GARDEN c1965 E5196

The Helen Garden, opened in September 1933, was given to the town by the late Mrs Helen Reid Stewart Hornby Lewis, as a plaque informs us. The hedges, plantings, paths and the thatched pavilions have strikingly civilised what was a windswept bare grass area. Beyond are the late Victorian buildings of St Bede's Preparatory School.

EASTBOURNE, HOLYWELL RETREAT 1910 62956

Looking towards Beachy Head, this view shows the 'combe' of Holy Well with its paths. It is here that the sea can be reached, albeit by a steep path, in a break in the cliffs enlarged by quarrying. The scene is unrecognisable now, as trees and plantings have matured to remove the bleakness of this Edwardian view.

HOLYWELL c1955 E5193
Eventually the steep paths lead down to the sea at Holy Well where sea bathing is possible, although the notice warns that it is dangerous when the red flag is flying. The beach huts of curiously railway style have long gone and are now replaced by modern toilets, but the fine views of the chalk cliffs remain.

HOLYWELL 1925 77957
By 1925 Holywell had acquired a pantiled tea room, the Holywell Tea Chalet, with a loggia and tables on the lawns. Nowadays, the loggia has been replaced by a flat-roofed extension and the lawns by low-maintenance crazy paving. The vegetation on the slopes behind and along the steep paths is now dense.

HOLYWELL 1925 77959
The combe, an area of flat ground and in fact an old chalk quarry, was laid out with garden beds, walks and loggias. The far one remains intact and is dated 1922. The left-hand one has since had a pergola or loggia added.

PARADISE 1910 62957
The road climbs here along the chalk amid the beech woods of the Paradise Plantation. It picturesquely linked the old town with Meads, and was a popular stroll for visitors. The lay-by where the children posed is still there; to the right is now the Royal Eastbourne golf course of 1887.

WILLINGDON, THE DOWNS C1955 W446019

Heading north from Eastbourne, you turn left in Willingdon to climb Butt Lane to the Downs. This view at Butt Brow north-west towards Combe Hill across Willingdon Bottom is part of the four thousand acres that the corporation of Eastbourne bought in 1929 to conserve for the citizens and posterity.

POLEGATE, THE DOWNS C1955 P259033

Walk a couple of hundred yards further north along Butts Brow and you can look out north-eastwards across The Combe and its disused quarry past the suburban spread of Polegate and Willingdon to long views across the Weald of Sussex.

POLGATE, THE ROAD TO JEVINGTON C1955 P259016

Back into Willingdon, continue north to turn towards Jevington, through Wannock, and onto the scenic Jevington Road. This village view looks north past Street Farm on the right, and although the big barn on the right has gone, the houses all remain. The church is famed for the Jevington Slab, a curious Anglo-Saxon sculptural relief of Christ.

EAST DEAN
The Village Green c1955 E136060

Continuing south, cross the Eastbourne to
Seaford road into the centre of East Dean village
with its steep winding lanes. The village has a most
attractive Norman church somewhat off-centre
and south-east of the village green. To the right
can be seen The Dipperays, a fine Georgian
mansion with a curious name.

EAST DEAN, THE WAR MEMORIAL 1921 71402
On a sunny weekend day the customers of The Tiger Inn, out of view to the right and very popular with walkers, spill onto the green and bring it vigorously to life. This view is remarkably unchanged, although the then new War Memorial has weathered and is now surrounded by railings.

WEST DEAN
1921

The village lies north of the Seaford road, which crosses the Cuckmere River at Exceat. On its no-through road in a short valley leading to the Cuckmere River, it feels amazingly isolated amid the Friston Forest. To the left of the church tower is the Old Parsonage, a 13th-century house of great interest.

◆

SEAFORD
The Esplanade 1906

Once a proud member of the medieval Cinque Ports, various attempts to revive the town as a seaside resort half succeeded. The Esplanade represents one such attempt after the railway arrived in 1864, but sadly only two of these imposing late-Victorian terraces survive.

WEST DEAN 1921 71401

SEAFORD, THE ESPLANADE 1906 55661

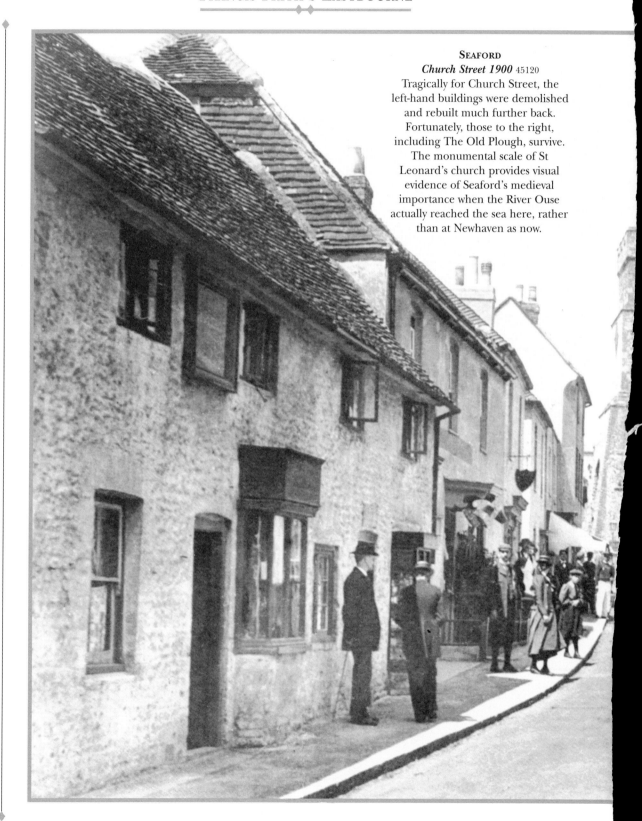

SEAFORD
Church Street 1900 45120
Tragically for Church Street, the left-hand buildings were demolished and rebuilt much further back. Fortunately, those to the right, including The Old Plough, survive. The monumental scale of St Leonard's church provides visual evidence of Seaford's medieval importance when the River Ouse actually reached the sea here, rather than at Newhaven as now.

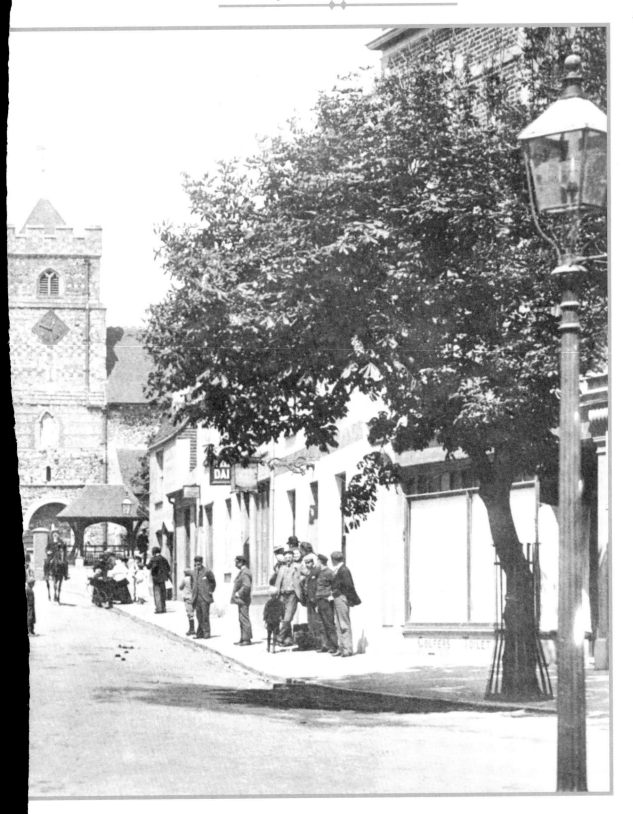

SEAFORD, HIGH STREET 1890 27771

This tranquil view has changed much since 1890. The treed gardens, the walls and the houses to the right were replaced in 1894 by a three-storey parade of shops, while the Old Tree Hotel on the corner of Broad Street was replaced in the 1960s. The building closing the vista has also been lost.

SEAFORD, LULLINGTON HILL 1894 34497

On the east bank of the Cuckmere River opposite Alfriston, Lullington is very much a shrunken medieval village, with its isolated church a good quarter of a mile north of Lullington Court, the farm complex in the middle distance. Beyond, a white horse was cut into the downland chalk in the 19th century by a James Pagden.

ALFRISTON, THE OLD CLERGY HOUSE 1921 71427
Almost ruinous when acquired by the National Trust as its first building in 1896, the clergy house was carefully restored. Situated on The Tye, the village green, by the fine parish church, it is an oak framed 'Wealden house' of about 1380, in which the projecting end bays and central open hall are under one continuous roof.

ALFRISTON, MARKET SQUARE 1921 71426
The church and Clergy House lie closer to the river, while the village, completely unspoilt, runs north-south along higher ground. The place was a notorious smuggling centre; the tile-hung house on the left is Ye Olde Smugglers Inne, in the 18th century the house of Stanton Collins, one of Alfriston's leading smugglers.

ALFRISTON
High Street 1921 71422
Apart from the visitors' cars, the High Street is unchanged. The richly timber-framed 15th-century George and Dragon on the left is a highlight; beyond is the Square, with its 15th-century market cross. Off the street are numerous narrow alleys between the houses, in Sussex known as Twittens, and probably useful to smugglers.

UPPER DICKER, THE DICKER c1955 U50018
Head towards Hailsham, avoiding the A22, and you pass through the oddly named Upper Dicker, mostly an Edwardian estate village. At the crossroads stands The Dicker, a somewhat eclectic and odd mansion of 1908, now St Bede's School. This was built for the notorious MP, Horatio Bottomley, jailed for fraud in 1922, in nouveau-riche medieval-cum-Swiss chalet style.

UPPER DICKER, THE PLOUGH INN c1955 U50004
This Shepherd Neame pub pre-dates Horatio Bottomley's era, and includes 18th- and earlier 19th-century elements. Much of the brick is now painted, and the 'lych gate' roof can be seen next to the inn sign. Beyond are the walls to the grounds of The Dicker, but many of the trees are now gone.

UPPER DICKER C1955 U50017
The hedge at the right belongs to the churchyard of Holy Trinity, a somewhat unattractive Neo-Norman church of 1843. The main street runs north lined with estate cottages of around 1900, which seem to have been built on the village green. Since the 1950s the village shop has transferred to the middle distance, near the van.

HAILSHAM, GEORGE STREET 1899 44957
Looking along George Street from Market Square, the timber-framed building and Ellis's were replaced in 1910 in Jacobean style by Market Chambers and a bank. This view captures the flavour of old Hailsham, nicknamed The String Town for its Victorian industries of sack, rope and twine manufacture.

HAILSHAM
High Street 1902 48483
There is enough of old Hailsham surviving to make a
visit worthwhile, but it has to be admitted that this
part of the High Street has suffered greatly. Beyond
Parkers, all has gone, replaced by a modern shopping
centre, while to the right the tree has gone, and all
the houses are now shops.

PEVENSEY, THE CASTLE 1894 34477

On 28 September 1066 William, Duke of Normandy, landed here and occupied the long-abandoned Roman fortress, which then occupied a promontory overlooking open sea. From here he moved to the place now known as Battle, and conquered England by defeating King Harold at the Battle of Hastings. In fact, the viewpoint here was in the sea until medieval times.

PEVENSEY, THE CASTLE ENTRANCE 1890 25339

The fortress, named Anderida, was built in the 4th century AD as one of the Saxon Shore Forts to defend Roman Britannia from Saxon raiders. In the middle ages the port was one of the Cinque Ports, before the sea turned to marshes. The castle was restored in the 1930s: the ivy has long gone.

PEVENSEY, THE VILLAGE C1955 P50051

South-east of Pevensey proper is the amorphous mass of Pevensey Bay. There are a few older houses on Sea Road, and on the right is the Bay Hotel of 1899. The settlement grew up at the end of the shingle spits that cut Pevensey off from the sea to create the great wetlands of the Levels.

PEVENSEY, THE VILLAGE C1965 P50085

Round the corner to the Eastbourne Road, with The Bay Hotel on the right, the architectural quality drops sharply to typical seaside nowhere. Many buildings have been replaced by 1960s and 1970s three-storey blocks of flats, and in the middle distance is St. Wilfred's Church, a 1968 building that adds little to Pevensey Bay's character.

Index

FRITH PRODUCTS & SERVICES

Francis Frith would doubtless be pleased to know that the pioneering publishing venture he started in 1860 still continues today. More than a hundred and thirty years later, The Francis Frith Collection continues in the same innovative tradition and is now one of the foremost publishers of vintage photographs in the world. Some of the current activities include:

Interior Decoration

Today Frith's photographs can be seen framed and as giant wall murals in thousands of pubs, restaurants, hotels, banks, retail stores and other public buildings throughout the country. In every case they enhance the unique local atmosphere of the places they depict and provide reminders of gentler days in an increasingly busy and frenetic world.

Product Promotions

Frith products have been used by many major companies to promote the sales of their own products or to reinforce their own history and heritage. Brands include Hovis bread, Courage beers, Scots Porage Oats, Colman's mustard, Cadbury's foods, Mellow Birds coffee, Dunhill pipe tobacco, Guinness, and Bulmer's Cider.

Genealogy and Family History

As the interest in family history and roots grows world-wide, more and more people are turning to Frith's photographs of Great Britain for images of the towns, villages and streets where their ancestors lived; and, of course, photographs of the churches and chapels where their ancestors were christened, married and buried are an essential part of every genealogy tree and family album.

A series of easy-to-use CD Roms is planned for publication, and an increasing number of Frith photographs will be able to be viewed on specialist genealogy sites. A growing range of Frith books will be available on CD.

The Internet

Already thousands of Frith photographs can be viewed and purchased on the internet. By the end of the year 2000 some 60,000 Frith photographs will be available on the internet. The number of sites is constantly expanding, each focussing on different products and services from the Collection.

Some of the sites are listed below.

www.townpages.co.uk
www.familystorehouse.com
www.britannia.com
www.icollector.com
www.barclaysquare.co.uk
www.cornwall-online.co.uk

For background information on the Collection look at the two following sites:

www.francisfrith.com
www.francisfrith.co.uk

Frith Products

All Frith photographs are available Framed or just as Mounted Prints, and can be ordered from the address below. From time to time other products - Address Books, Calendars, Table Mats, Postcards etc - are available.

The Frith Collectors' Guild

In response to the many customers who enjoy collecting Frith photographs we have created the Frith Collectors' Guild. Members are entitled to a range of benefits, including a regular magazine, special discounts and special limited edition products.

For further information: if you would like further information on any of the above aspects of the Frith business please contact us at the address below:

The Francis Frith Collection, Frith's Barn, Teffont, Salisbury, Wiltshire England SP3 5QP.
Tel: +44 (0) 1722 716 376 Fax: +44 (0) 1722 716 881 Email: frithbook.co.uk

Frith Book Co 1999 Titles

From 2000 we aim at publishing 100 new books each year. For latest catalogue please contact Frith Book Co

Barnstaple	1-85937-084-5	£12.99	Oct 99	Maidstone	1-85937-056-X	£12.99	Sep 99
Blackpool	1-85937-049-7	£12.99	Sep 99	Northumberland & Tyne and Wear	1-85937-072-1	£14.99	Sep 99
Bognor Regis	1-85937-055-1	£12.99	Sep 99	North Yorkshire	1-85937-048-9	£14.99	Sep 99
Bristol	1-85937-050-0	£12.99	Sep 99	Nottingham	1-85937-060-8	£12.99	Sep 99
Cambridge	1-85937-092-6	£12.99	Oct 99	Oxfordshire	1-85937-076-4	£14.99	Oct 99
Cambridgeshire	1-85937-086-1	£14.99	Nov 99	Penzance	1-85937-069-1	£12.99	Sep 99
Cheshire	1-85937-045-4	£14.99	Sep 99	Reading	1-85937-087-X	£12.99	Nov 99
Chester	1-85937-090-X	£12.99	Nov 99	St Ives	1-85937-068-3	£12.99	Sep 99
Chesterfield	1-85937-071-3	£12.99	Sep 99	Salisbury	1-85937-091-8	£12.99	Nov 99
Chichester	1-85937-089-6	£12.99	Nov 99	Scarborough	1-85937-104-3	£12.99	Sep 99
Cornwall	1-85937-054-3	£14.99	Sep 99	Scottish Castles	1-85937-077-2	£14.99	Oct 99
Cotswolds	1-85937-099-3	£14.99	Nov 99	Sevenoaks and Tonbridge	1-85937-057-8	£12.99	Sep 99
				Sheffield and S Yorkshire	1-85937-070-5	£12.99	Sep 99
				Shropshire	1-85937-083-7	£14.99	Nov 99
				Southampton	1-85937-088-8	£12.99	Nov 99
				Staffordshire	1-85937-047-0	£14.99	Sep 99
				Stratford upon Avon	1-85937-098-5	£12.99	Nov 99
				Suffolk	1-85937-074-8	£14.99	Oct 99
				Surrey	1-85937-081-0	£14.99	Oct 99
				Torbay	1-85937-063-2	£12.99	Sep 99
				Wiltshire	1-85937-053-5	£14.99	Sep 99

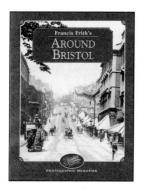
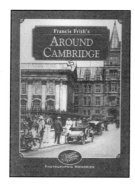

Derby	1-85937-046-2	£12.99	Sep 99
Devon	1-85937-052-7	£14.99	Sep 99
Dorset	1-85937-075-6	£14.99	Oct 99
Dorset Coast	1-85937-062-4	£14.99	Sep 99
Dublin	1-85937-058-6	£12.99	Sep 99
East Anglia	1-85937-059-4	£14.99	Sep 99
Eastbourne	1-85937-061-6	£12.99	Sep 99
English Castles	1-85937-078-0	£14.99	Oct 99
Essex	1-85937-082-9	£14.99	Nov 99
Falmouth	1-85937-066-7	£12.99	Sep 99
Hampshire	1-85937-064-0	£14.99	Sep 99
Hertfordshire	1-85937-079-9	£14.99	Nov 99
Isle of Man	1-85937-065-9	£14.99	Sep 99
Liverpool	1-85937-051-9	£12.99	Sep 99

British Life A Century Ago

246 x 189mm 144pp, hardback. Black and white Lavishly illustrated with photos from the turn of the century, and with extensive commentary. It offers a unique insight into the social history and heritage of bygone Britain.

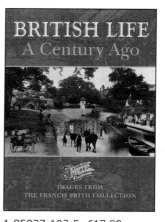

1-85937-103-5 £17.99 ....

Available from your local bookshop or from the publisher

To receive your FREE Mounted Print

Cut out this Voucher and return it with your remittance for £1.50 to cover postage and handling. Choose any photograph included in this book. Your SEPIA print will be A4 in size, and mounted in a cream mount with burgundy rule lines, overall size 14 x 11 inches.

Order additional Mounted Prints at HALF PRICE (only £7.49 each*)

If there are further pictures you would like to order, possibly as gifts for friends and family, acquire them at half price (no additional postage and handling required).

Have your Mounted Prints framed*

For an additional £14.95 per print you can have your chosen Mounted Print framed in an elegant polished wood and gilt moulding, overall size 16 x 13 inches (no additional postage and handling required).

---

* IMPORTANT!
These special prices are only available if ordered using the original voucher on this page (no copies permitted) and at the same time as your free Mounted Print, for delivery to the same address

---

Frith Collectors' Guild

From time to time we publish a magazine of news and stories about Frith photographs and further special offers of Frith products. If you would like 12 months FREE membership, please return this form and we will send you a New Member Pack.

Send completed forms to:
**The Francis Frith Collection,
Frith's Barn, Teffont, Salisbury,
Wiltshire SP3 5QP**

Voucher for FREE and Reduced Price Frith Prints

Picture no.	Page number	Qty	Mounted @ £7.49	Framed + £14.95	Total Cost
		1	**Free of charge***	£	£
			£	£	£
			£	£	£
			£	£	£
			£	£	£
			£	£	£

Title: AROUND EASTBOURNE
061-6

* Post & handling	£1.50
Total Order Cost	£

Please do not photocopy this voucher. Only the original is valid, so please cut it out and return it to us.

I enclose a cheque / postal order for £ . . . .
made payable to 'The Francis Frith Collection'
OR please debit my Mastercard / Visa / Switch / Amex card

Number . . . .

Expires . . . . Signature . . . .

Name Mr/Mrs/Ms . . . .

Address . . . .

. . . .

. . . .

. . . . Postcode . . . .

Daytime Tel No . . . .   Valid to 31/12/01

The Francis Frith Collectors' Guild

I would like to receive the New Members Pack offering 12 months FREE membership.
061-6

Name Mr/Mrs/Ms . . . .

Address . . . .

. . . .

. . . .

. . . . Postcode . . . .